A Quietus

Josephine Lay

Black Eyes Publishing UK

A Quietus
By Josephine Lay

© Josephine Lay 2021

Published by Black Eyes Publishing UK, 2021
Brockworth, Gloucestershire, England
www.blackeyespublishinguk.co.uk

ISBN: 9781913195151

Josephine Lay has asserted her moral right under the Copyright, Designs and Patents Act, 1988, to be identified as the author of this work.

All Rights reserved. No part of this publication may be reproduced, copied, stored in a retrieval system, or transmitted, in any form or by any means, without the prior written consent of the copyright holder, nor be otherwise circulated in any form of binding or cover other than that in which it is published and without a similar condition being imposed on the subsequent purchaser.

A CIP catalogue record for this title is available from the British Library.

Cover Painting: Pennie Elfick
                 www.pennieelfick.co.uk

Cover design: Jason Conway, The Daydream Academy.
                 www.thedaydreamacademy.com

Dedicated to

the memory of my parents:

Ena Harriot Crossley

Alan William Leslie Crossley

Other collections by this author

Poetry

Inside Reality

Unravelling

Short Stories

Saffron Tones

'Dying is a wild night and a new road.'

Emily Dickenson

'Death may be the greatest of all human blessings.'

Socrates

Contents

11 Civilisation
12 Sewn Up
13 Pyronia Tithonus
14 Stepping Stones
15 Don't Focus on the Mask
16 Climate Change
17 The Last Cut of Summer
18 Cotswold Life
19 Dad
20 It is October
21 Abscission
22 Magic
23 A strange topography
24 The nursery
25 Room in New York
27 Squatting
28 In a Home
30 Memory with Elgar
31 A Quietus
32 Father
33 For Death is a woman
34 Sallekhana at Epiphany
36 In Memoriam
37 Half-life
38 Take up the newly dead
39 Womb
40 Still Life
41 The Reader
42 Warrior
43 Altered Realities 2020
44 Monogamy Becomes a Heavy Load

45 Branding Iron
46 Sparks
47 Brief Encounter
48 The Mould
49 Medusa in Love
50 The Herbalist
51 The Enlightenment of Stones
52 Blood of Gods
53 Am I a coward
54 Distanced
55 Windfalls
56 Quietus
57 Hoarfrost
58 On this Winter path
59 Grave Goods
60 Armageddon
61 Staged

63 Josephine Biography
65 Acknowledgements
67 Complete Quotes

A Quietus

Civilisation

Hunting beneath the hot sun
or fishing under a full moon
brings little rest

but when there is food in plenty
and the roof of the hut lets in no rain

when your spear is laid down by the fire
and the log pile will last the night

when your fishing net is mended
and there are furs to wrap against cold

then it is time to contemplate the stars.

Sewn Up

Brick walls and fences hem me in
the fabric of civilisation
folds around me
seams me into shape.

Patterns designed at birth
pinned into place
tacked and stitched
presented with mannequin smile.

I reach for the scissors
cut away the frills
unlace the corset

step naked into the wild and run.

I will be caught
sewn back into line.

But I will break out again.

Pyronia Tithonus

I've left my garden to grow wild
let dandelions and willowherb thrive
bindweed twines stem of shrub and rose
and now the Gatekeepers have come
to settle behind the high fences
to keep watch on those who enter.

They welcome in hedgehogs, thrushes,
wasps and ladybirds: all creatures
that prey on pests or scavenge waste.
The Gatekeepers land on bushes
lay their eggs on the tall grasses
leave their children to roam at will.

At the arrival of late summer,
I'll watch the splitting of chrysalis
and the slow filling of wing.

There is shelter in this rough order
and the Gatekeepers recognise
how civilisation suffocates.

Stepping Stones

I used stepping stones to cross
felt warm rock under cold feet

left footprints.

But the boulders shifted
under the flooding stream.

The ford becomes less clear
phrases overflow the page.

The challenge is:

to step on words as steady as stone
they'll keep you safe as waters rise.

Don't Focus on the Mask

Deep beneath this flesh and bone
a snake sleeps curled about my spine
quiescent, lulled by my heart's beat.

Body language belies the truth
on the mask of my face
no trace of his existence
no clues in tone of voice
but sumptuous syllables
slip from my pen as he uncoils.

I feel his sleek body writhe
sense his slithering slide into vein
know his primaeval power.

Climate Change

The August sun beats down
on the turning trees
and we, still on holiday,
find yellow leaves in the
swimming pool each morning.

These early Autumn shades
strike sombre shadows.
We do not swim again
for the rest of our stay.

The Last Cut of Summer

I mow the lawn, pausing to empty
fresh cuttings onto the compost heap
they cover the dying with sliced life.
Three silver birches stand at the end
of the garden - these whispering sisters
are so close their roots inter-mesh
their crowns touch as the wind passes.

Birds twitter on branches, leaves rustle
but I don't speak either language
and these voices of Nature are soon
drowned by the noise of machinery.
I wonder if grass screams as the blade
cuts: its collective voice at too high
a register for the human ear.

Later, as leaves turn ochre and gold
the silver of birch bark shines through.
On the lowest branches hang secrets
hidden by last Summer's foliage.

They dangle like votive offerings:
a nest in the crook of a branch
an old sock hanging by its toe
a child's hair-ribbon, the blue fading
strips of polythene flapping like ghosts
the tail-feather of a crow glinting
black iridescence.

Cotswold Life

That Autumn the woodlice invaded.
We would clear them away
but next morning they'd return
to feast on the rotten wood at the base
of our doorstep.

A few at first, then more came
as though invitations
had been sent out for this banquet.

During the Summer we'd renovated,
carpeted and perfected our décor.

Furnished with plush sofas and chairs
hung modern art on white walls
bought glossy magazines:
Vogue, Tatler and House & Garden
to place on our new, glass coffee tables.

Nonetheless, our Cotswold façade
was unable to prevent this army of Nature
gnawing away at the base
of our content.

Dad

your painting hangs on my wall
I see it each morning -
in Autumn it comes alive.

The shallow stream under beech trees
copper leaves floating on water.
In the distance
pale hills, distant as memories.

That day
I returned home unexpectedly
found you creating a new picture
while this spiral of parchment
lay in the waste paper basket

rejected for a mis-painted branch.

I rescued it.
Later, unfurled its stiff edges

marvelled at the discarded masterpiece.

It is October

and cooling air descends on the *heron-priested* shore.
Head lowered, coat billowing like a spinnaker
you trudge the wooded paths
below these wet Welsh hills.

You walk through narrow streets of the grey town
where gossips lean on fences, wagging tongues
the very place where you found your language.

The retracing of steps spurs a wish
to keep to wedding vows
to stop leaning on beer-swilled bars.

But these resolves you know will falter
when, shipwrecked midst concrete and glass,
you'll drown homesickness in ice cold beer
and grasp hold of love like a lifebelt.

*Originally written as a letter for the 'Dylan' competition
by Indigo Dreams 2020 - rewritten as a poem.*

Abscission

Deep in deciduous forests
listen to
the singing of leaves

as Death clothes
them in the raiment of Kings.

Here is no grim reaper
scythe in hand.

See her dance between the trees
her golden cloak flying
her feet scattering the fallen leaves.

This then is the zenith of life
this moment of dying.

Praise the wrinkling of skin
the dulling of eye
the whitening of hair.

Learn to fall gracefully
gilded by the folds of her cloak.

Magic

There are moments when
I find it in the perfume of flowers
in the sunlight breaking through dark clouds
in the song of a passing bird.

There are days when I search for it
under stones, in bramble thickets and log piles,
in puddles, drains and culverts,
below the green waters of a pond.

There are nights, when I know not to look
when I lose belief and see only darkness.

Then, like a blessing, it fills my dreams.

A strange topography

with shifts of impression that adjust the view.

Light flickers from between bound pages
settles on the shadow shapes that rise
from a base line.

Watch the feet, uncertain, placing weight
between tortured trees
whose strange fruits spoil.

Dead leaves accumulate -
a mulch for the fertile mind
where seeds are planted

by a child playing the adult
hesitant, furtive. Ignorant

of so many concepts
that float above in grey skies.

On the ground sharp rocks
and gravel cut and draw blood.
A contrast to the soft grass

at the entrance of caves where drips
of sentiment have formed
stalactites of past pain.

The nursery

was full of many toys:
drums and whirling tops
dolls and toy soldiers
a whistle and a tambourine

she could have been a one-man band
but she was always told
to be quiet.

Soft toys lay on wooden building blocks
a train, a slate, some paint
but no paper or chalk -
nothing seemed to fit together.

She asked questions
but the soldiers wouldn't answer
the dolls lay dumb - eyes wide open.

The train only moved in one direction
the circle was closed, the points broken.
She pumped the spinning top
waited to see where it would fall -

wondered if the world
would make more sense
when it stopped spinning.

Room in New York
from the painting of the same name by Edward Hopper

A yellow rectangle in a black stone wall
captures my attention   forks direction.

This frame of lode-stone   attracts and repels
loitering between these two forces   I am static
looking in on the scene   a voyeur.

Two figures strapped   in this flat room-scape
a man in shirtsleeves sat in a bloated arm chair
a woman in a red gown   leaning on a piano.

One finger poised above a note   hesitating
her gaze avoiding the score   projecting the tedium of evening
his retreat behind a broadsheet.

She hits the note like the stroke of a metronome
monotone   white light falls on her bare arms
skin bleached   leached of life.

The man does not look up   raises the paper higher
a fragile barrier   but one she can't climb over or under
this scarlet bird in a canary yellow room.

Behind her the door is shut   a russet rectangle towering
ready to open   if she'd turn the handle   put on dancing shoes
collect her coat   put the red back in her veins.

He disdains to look at her   focuses
his quarry on the printed page   across a round table
they exist   on the circumference.

Her finger stops   no frisson in fabric of her dress
I'm so close   if she looked   she'd see my breath
upon the glass.

Squatting

A crab scuttles in the shallows, hides
behind rocks, intent on acquiring
a new shell in which to live.

A long line of crabs hurry for dwellings
when one residence is left empty
a crab discards his home and climbs in.

At each new address I move in my bed
bring chairs and tables to be illumined
by the light through different windows.

I try the interior for size, spread self
into corners, glad to settle by the hearth -
merely an extra in this film of house

while the clock ticks away the minutes
till I move on.

In a Home

When he sits in his chair by the window
my father's head shines in the sun
like a hard-boiled egg.

There's even a dip in his skull
where someone's put a spoon
to open his cranium.

This was the surgeon who broke
through to the yolk
and scooped out the soft mass
of the tumour.

When he sits in his chair by the window
my father's head droops to his chest
as he snores after lunch
while he waits for me to visit.

As I arrive, I see his pale pate
through glass, fine hairs knotted
into a silver halo.

I walk towards him, take his hand
from beneath an ill-fitting cardigan
that doesn't belong to him,
and greet him with a kiss.

He raises his head
looks at the clock on the wall

lances me with a glance
as sharp as a spear

and smiling, says
'You're eight minutes late.'

Memory with Elgar

I remember the cold night air
the church pews like stone
the tableau set before the altar
Christus Rex.

I watched our breath rising to rafters
my father standing in one corner
ready to press play
on the tape recorder.

The bite of the cello
cutting through dim light
the score played by the fingers
of Jaqueline Dupre.

I wondered at the raw emotion
and how he fed this music in between
the script, like a conductor
I'd never met before.

A Quietus
(Oxford Dictionary def.: *Something that has a calming or soothing effect.*)

A quietus is the falling
into the space between notes.

A quietus is absence:
a track after a train has passed
a landscape free of people.

The relaxing of tired muscle
the pausing for breath.

A quietus is stillness after storm:
the dropping of wind
the drying of ground.

The smoothness between ripples
on the surface of water.

A quietus is a sleeping beast:
felt pads between talons
skin beneath the fur

a yawn of sharp jaws.

Father

your mind was fettered by the everyday
truncated by criticism from those around you
who only saw one way to be.

Inside your skull, your brain, when left alone,
addressed multiple points of view
and saw far beyond the everyday.

Your thoughts caused you to search
the star lit skies; you viewed the
milky way through telescopes.

Absorbing knowledge and applying it
you understood the universe
as far as you were able.

Frail in health from polio, with a tumour
the size of a small orange in your brain
you still read and discussed.

Dust you became, but it wouldn't have concerned you.
You always wanted to return to the everlasting cycle.

For Death is a woman

her ebony arms folded beneath her cloak.
This lonely shadow

walks close behind
her footsteps are silent.

Her breath is fresh air: she is easy to miss

till she presses the warmth of her body
through her dusty clothes.

When she opens her arms, the cloak is held wide
showing nothing but blackness.

Embraced in its folds, see on her hooded face
the trace of a smile.

Sallekhana at Epiphany

Christmas Eve -
my mother's head upon a pillow as she makes
her choice: no medical intervention.

For weeks, every morsel of food
has made her sick
hot chocolate is her staple diet.

Her poor belly distended since
she suffered the surgeon's knife.
Nothing they do can make her better.

They say they'll feed her through a tube
that will enter a vein in her groin,
she groans at the thought.

I find a nursing home where staff
support her decision to neither eat
nor drink till the time comes.

She tells me she will live into the New year.
And she does.

When I take her hand for the last time
I feel her move *into that goodnight*
with no rage, fight or sorrow

and from eye's corner
I sense figures - arms open.

I am not sad, for joy halos
the space around us.

It is some time before the tears begin.

Sallekhana
In the Jain religion this is a spiritual height reached by the departed when death is embraced with calmness and peace. The person ceases to eat and the death is a tranquil process for everyone involved: it is also believed to end the cycle of Karma: there will be no further incarnations.

In Memoriam

The cold from stone seeps in through coats, gloves and booted feet. This memorial service for my mother is a sparse gathering; just a few of her friends, all aged, and frail. No one will attempt the steep winding road to the cemetery.

The priest and I make that journey. I clasp the urn of her ashes to my chest and as we climb the snow comes. The feathered flakes fall silently on my head and hands, deaden sound and whiten the path.

At the gates of the cemetery a man waits to inter her ashes under the marble plaque where my father's remains lie: they will be reunited.

We stand sheltered under a tall Cedar of Lebanon that spreads its dark branches. The curtain of snow blanks out the world, only this one small patch of green, where the stone is lifted: waiting.

Half-life

He feels her presence and her absence
in the dark hours.
Thick blackness paints the windows
in each room he sees it coat the house.

Drawing the curtains doesn't shut it out –
like pressure behind the eyes
closing the lids brings no relief.

From the bay window to the hall door
from the kitchen to the stairs, he prowls
a trapped beast in a black wrapped box
mind sharp, hackles high, wanting to howl.

There's no escaping this Indian ink as it oozes
under the door or in through the letterbox.

He turns on all the lights but the darkness
merely retreats into him, invades his mind,
this old adversary coats his soul
wraps it completely.

In the kitchen, he fills the kettle, flips the switch
waits for the note of its song - sees her special mug
remembers her fingers cupping its warmth.

Her hands were always cold.

Take up the newly dead

hold them close and carry them
for though they have left us
they are in need of love

are fragile without skin
shapeless without bones
and their breath is remembrance.

Womb

I walk to the isolated shore along
a narrow road that leads down from the hills.

The force of the wind is constant -
I lean as it tears breath from lungs.

Out in the bay, mounds of water roll, crests spuming
on the sand, waves break in a torrent of foam
while the gravel roars.

Strands of hair cling to my damp cheeks
and at sea's edge I leave footprints.

The pull of the moon is strong and we are filled:
the sea with numberless progeny

me with just one.

Still Life

A room in twilight.

Patio door shut against bitter cold
snow-light on pale walls
shadows across carpets.

Where she sits, a lamp pools yellow
illuminating white paper
and her hand holding a pencil.

Her fingers, fluidly precise,
mark out the essence of
fruit bowl and broken vase

her hair tucked behind ears
as she bends to her art.

Elsewhere in the house:
a washing machine spins
a door closes - footsteps fade

and out of the silence -
the scratching of graphite.

The Reader
for Thomas Trofimuk

This woman is in love with a new man
who has entered her life,
though they have never met.

A man who writes
and as she reads his words, she knows him.

His phrases have a heavy perfume
of musk, thyme and rosemary.

His punctuation thrills her skin as she waits
for the qualification of a statement, a concept,
an emotion.

The font on the page is Garamond

and his stories are like her dreams.
She returns to her bed, opens to the next
chapter: eager for what is to come.

Outside the window, snow falls gently.

Thomas Trofimuk is a Canadian novelist and poet.
In part of his novel 'THIS IS ALL A LIE' he writes about Garamond's life. The
type face for the novel is 'Garamond' – as is the font in this collection.
There is a recurring theme of snow, in much of Trofimuk's work.

Warrior

She writes:

pen sheathed
within a scabbard
of carved words.

Their grace
hides the thrust

only after
they are spoken
do you feel

the cut.

Altered Realities 2020

Some novelist has added me into his plot
typed me into the pages of his book
and not as the central character.

A puppeteer, expertly tweaking strings
has made me dance to his choreography
I will collapse when the show is over.

Certainty is seeping from the picture
in which I am framed. Shown in this gallery
I can look out, but few stop to view me.

I am cut into cubes, placed into a distorted
perspective I cannot correct.
I try not to slip into the shadows.

I struggle to express my state of mind
within this limited paradigm.

And alas, I can help no one.

Monogamy Becomes a Heavy Load

No longer a swan mirrored on smooth water
my tousled feathers have a scarlet tinge.

You glide contented through the days
relaxed - you do not see me struggle.

You dabble in the shallows, head lowered
then raised: water dripping from your beak.

I paddle furiously against strong currents
that entice me out towards the weir.

When I finally surrender and follow instinct
the water of the lake will reflect my absence.

The Branding Iron

The touch of her hand on your arm
burns you

and you know that piece of skin
will always feel different.

Her skirt strokes your knee
as she turns and you inhale her perfume.

You ask her to stay, to have another drink.
She smiles at you with sympathetic eyes
and you feel pitied.

You know she can't reciprocate
kindness is all she will offer.

Suddenly you wish she would leave
though the warmth of her body
ignites you.

You could so easily hate her
for not giving in -

for not loving you back.

Sparks

We wove dreams in air and inhaled them
held them close as the world slipped by.

Witch and Wizard, we dripped
love potions into each other's eyes.

Friends issued warnings and so did the trees
we remained blind to all but each other.

We lit our fire, huddled together, sang songs
not understanding that life might ignite

and leave only ashes.

Brief Encounter

Was our first meeting romantic?

The day was heavy with dark clouds
the smell of diesel was in my nose
and there wasn't a flower in sight.

An icy wind grasped at my throat
brought tears to my eyes, blurring vision
and there was no violin.

Since our meeting, the years
have been filled with the light of candles
on so many restaurant tables.

Our meeting wasn't romantic.
I never even caught your eye
as you passed by under your umbrella.

So why do I, so often
remember you?

The Mould

She thought him a god returned to Earth
coffee skin and chestnut eyes
with a smile that rose the sun.

His hands were generous, warm
mounds of Venus full and firm.
An Adonis with impeccable nails

when his hand touched hers
she melted and was cast.

Medusa in Love
an alternative version of events.

My sisters sleep while I protect and guard.
Many will say that I sleep too, not so.
I see him walk towards our cave, watch the gleam
of sunlight on his sword and shield, know my time
has come to be destroyed.

I love this youth
and lower my eyes, feeling no desire to curse.
I listen to the hissing of my hair
and know how monstrous I've become.

Gone the beauty with heavy tress
falling to waist, capturing the devotion of men
and the lust of Gods.

When Poseidon strode into the temple
I was curious. Did a moment of temptation
deserve such disgrace?

The young man's shadow passes petrified forms
of those who've dared to look.
He unsheathes his sword, I catch a glint of light
from the surface of his shield.
The snake heads writhe and spit -
venom dripping from their mouths.

But my heart grows as heavy as stone
and as his sword steadies for its stroke
I refuse to look upon his face.

The Herbalist

Fragrance leads her to each scented plant
growing beneath the inky Cedar trees
whose branches sieve the scattered stars.

Pale hands glint in the luminescence
fingers stroke the buds as she picks
aromatic leaves from the tips of stems.

She puts the precious herbs in the depths
of the black bag tied at her waist.
While her skirts brush the tall grasses

she gathers her harvest   at length
she stands tall   eyes closed   moonlight
tracing cheek bones   as she communes

becomes one with trees   senses a zephyr
rustle her dress as though she had leaves
believes she might stay like this perpetually

but the moon pales behind light cloud
halos out its radiance   ripples light
and Circe flows beneath its influence.

The Enlightenment of Stones

Consider the stones as they sit
as still as Buddhas, contemplating
the weight of gravity.

Stones suffer in their development
some are forged in fire

some are pressured into hardness
by the movement of tectonic plates

others are shaped by water
or cracked by ice.

When they find a place to settle
stones have no desire to move –
moss or no moss.

Adopt the silence of stone
the stillness of rock

let thought drift across hills of time
and stalagmites form in the caves of mind.

Sit like stones,
content to be.

Blood of Gods

Earth longs for moisture -
parched plants weep oil.

In the morning, the first fine rain
mists hills to blue

brings a sweet scent –
petrichor.

Am I a coward

to run from images of pain?

Children in poverty, cowering
from anger like kicked curs.

Women trapped bird-like
behind the cages of front doors.

The sick dying alone in aseptic tents
hands grasping the gloved fingers
of nurses who sweat under plastic gowns.

Am I a coward
to dive into the soft green of spring
to drown in birdsong?

I am a coward
lost and confused
like the rest of the world.

I am a coward, seeking survival.

Distanced

We've been left to tick tock down
to unwind as pointed hands slow.

We've been shunted onto sidings
left to rust outside of town

where winds shift the sands of time.
How slowly they rise?

But soon they'll flow in
and bury us.

Windfalls

The pears ripen slowly on the window ledge.
Late-Summer storms ripped them from trees.
Battered and bruised they may still taste sweet
these un-weaned pups - early orphaned.

Our children ripen behind closed windows.
Viral storms have ripped them from schools.
They stay 'safe' at home and draw rainbows
these lockdown kids - bereft of friends.

Quietus
(Oxford Dictionary def.: *Death or something that causes death, regarded as a release from life.*)

When they are released from life
where do the dead reside?

They cunningly conceal that loss of mass
as they slide from the body
into the immensity between stars.

They slip into the space between atoms
beneath layers of skin, along shafts of bone
deep in the belly of muscle.

They wait in the atrium of the heart
invisible, weightless -
till we in turn drop

into the darkness between matter.

Hoarfrost

A bitter cold has come and stands outside my door
it frosts the key, burns fingers as I try to turn the lock
I will not open but the chill seeps through the glass.
I stand silent, brain hunting a scheme to escape.
I knew there'd come a moment
I thought myself prepared.

A bitter cold has come and stands outside my door
my mind plays memories of heat, of light, of fire -
swimming in Cyprus; how the beach burned our feet.
Our campfire in the mountains under starry skies.
I knew there'd come a moment
but I thought myself prepared.

A bitter chill then came to stand outside our tent
we made love while the sun rose high above the clouds
our bodies warm in sleeping bags: our last sleep
before we trekked our different ways into the world.
I knew there'd be a moment
I hoped myself prepared.

A bitter cold has come and stands outside my door
it frosts the key, burns fingers as I try to turn the lock
if I open to the icy touch of death, will memories
keep out the cold; warm this inescapable moment
I knew was bound to come
though still, I'm unprepared.

On this Winter path

we walk by stark skeletons of trees.
Between their trunks

low light falls through mist
like sheets of shimmering glass.

Shadows cut the heaps of leaves
lying beneath our feet.

Hand in hand, we tread
the diminishing perspective

towards a vanishing point.

Up ahead I'll have to let you go
up ahead you will leave me.

Up ahead you will wait
in the gold mists of sunsets

till I can join you.

Grave Goods

Somewhere far out, on wild hill or plain
dig deep in soft soil, place me with love
beneath a sapling of a silver birch.

Bury me with no shroud, no Sunday best
lay me down on moist earth as in a crib
and set a stone to pillow my head.

Leave on my finger your single gold ring
and put your silver pendant at my throat.

Shake petals on my eyes to aid my sleep
then lower the tree's embracing roots
return the soil and tread us firmly down.

Together we'll lie under wind and rain.
I will slowly decline and the tree will take
my atoms to form leaflets at its crown.

Armageddon

We knitted up a storm
slipped threads of greed over needles

increased the stiches
till our blanket smothered the World.

Now we call on past gods
to help us

in this mesh of cupidity
that we must unravel

lest we suffocate.

Staged

The sun drips blood onto reflective surfaces
windows catch fire, white cliffs rouge.

Tinged crimson, dark clouds build across water
flashes of lightening cut the leaden grey
and no birds soar.

Even the gnats are silent as they dance
above the oily surface of the lake.

Everything waits for the show to begin
the orchestra heavy with tympanum.

I no longer want my ringside seat
but I stay for the last bow of the sun.

Biography

Josephine Lay is a poet and author living mid-way between Gloucester and Cheltenham. She has a jnt. BA(Hons) in Creative Studies in Eng. & English Lit. and an MA in Creative Writing for Young People from Bath Spa University.

In 2018 Josephine had two falls: one in February and one in July, both resulting in concussion and a period of post-concussion syndrome in the Autumn of that year. This precipitated Josephine into writing poetry and she joined The Gloucestershire Poetry Society (GPS). She became host of 'Squawkers' – a lively, monthly poetry event in Cheltenham and since the Pandemic, Josephine hosts the online Zoom event, 'Crafty Crows', which has become highly successful and International.

In Jan 2020 Josephine became Director of Operations for the GPS. She is also Editor for Black Eyes Publishing UK.

Acknowledgements

Thank you to my fellow poets at the Gloucestershire Poetry Society (GPS) who've helped me on my poetic journey: particularly, Z. D. Dicks, aka Ziggy The Poet, founder of the GPS, who handed that poetry baby on to me in January 2020.

A special thank you goes to Anna Saunders, who has become a friend, a tutor and a mentor and has written a lovely quote for the back of this book.

My thanks also go to Angela France for her mentoring and for her supportive and incisive blurb for the back of this book.

Further thanks to David Clarke who has also kindly written me a sensitive quote for this collection.

My thanks go to Thomas Trofimuk for his kind blurb. It is my good fortune to be in communication with a novelist that I hold in such high esteem.

And many thanks to Pennie Elfick; a Somerset artist for allowing us to use her painting for the basis of this cover.

And finally, of course, my gratitude to my lover and publisher, Peter Lay, of Black Eyes Publishing UK.

Stepping Stones: The last two lines of this poem were exhibited within Luke Jerrum's 'Of Earth and Sky' poetry installation of Summer 2020.

In a Home: was published by 'Ink Sweat and Tears' October 2020.

Warrior & Blood of Gods: earlier versions of these poems have been accepted by Black Bough Poetry for publication in 2021.

Other poems within this collection have been published in various anthologies.

Complete Quotes

Josephine Lay's *A Quietus* is lyrical and sharply observed. The poems cover a range of subjects, which always seem to be seeking the balance between beauty and the inevitable darkness of decay, to 'reach for the scissors/ cut away the frills/ unlace the corset' ('Sewn Up'), to see the risk in truly living.

Angela France

Delicate yet fierce, spare yet multi layered this is an emotionally affecting collection written by a poet who affirms life by interrogating mortality. *A Quietus* is a lyrical and erudite lesson in surrender. In a series of nuanced and carefully crafted poems we discover ways to live, and to face death, and how, when we encounter the reaper - we must ' learn to fall gracefully/ gilded by the folds of her cloak', but not before 'grasping hold of love like a lifebelt'.

Anna Saunders

The lodestar of Josephine Lay's *A Quietus* is nature. In these meditations on forests, gardens, insects, crabs, stones, pears, flowers and birds, the poet helps us find solace, orientation and hope in the natural world. Carefully observed and vividly expressed, these poems speak of the constraints imposed upon us by human society and the desire for creative fulfilment, while always acknowledging our fragile mortal condition. The poems of remembrance for Lay's parents are particularly moving – here she explores the power of poetry to heal the loss of those we love, how it can 'hold them close and carry them'. This is a varied and engaging collection from a poet with a distinct voice.

David Clarke

Josephine Lay's poems are fearless intaglios that stir and disturb. They breathe with yearning and wonder. Like all great poets, she brings the full force of her curiosity to the question of what it is to be human.

Thomas Trofimuk, *Waiting for Columbus*

www.ingramcontent.com/pod-product-compliance
Lightning Source LLC
Chambersburg PA
CBHW071756080526
44588CB00013B/2257